Chimpanzees

By Sandra Donovan

Raintree

ANIMALS OF THE RAINFOREST

www.raintreepublishers.co.uk
Visit our website to find out more information about Raintree books.

To order:
☎ Phone 44 (0) 1865 888112
🖹 Send a fax to 44 (0) 1865 314091
🖥 Visit the Raintree Bookshop at www.raintreepublishers.co.uk to browse our catalogue and order online.

First published in Great Britain by Raintree Publishers, Halley Court, Jordan Hill, Oxford, OX2 8EJ, part of Harcourt Education.
Raintree is a registered trademark of Harcourt Education Ltd.

Originated by Dot Gradations
Printed and bound in China by South China Printing

ISBN 1 844 21114 2
07 06 05 04 03
10 9 8 7 6 5 4 3 2 1

British Library Cataloguing in Publication Data
Donovan, Sandra
1. Chimpanzees – Juvenile literature
2. Rainforest ecology – Juvenile literature
599.8'85
A catalogue for this book is available from the British Library.

Acknowledgements
The publishers would like to thank the following for permission to reproduce photographs:
Root Resources/Kenneth Fink, pp. **6, 14, 16, 22**; Anthony Mercieca, pp. **5, 27, 28–29**; A.J. Copley, pp. **1, 24**; Mark Newman, pp. **8, 21, 26**; Chris Crowley, pp. **11, 12**; Gerald Corsi, p. **18**.

Cover photograph reproduced with permission of Corbis/Tom Brakefield

Every effort has been made to contact copyright holders of any material reproduced in this book. Any omissions will be rectified in subsequent printings if notice is given to the publishers.

Contents

Any words appearing in the text in bold, **like this**, are explained in the Glossary.

Canary Islands
(SPAIN)

MOROCCO

TUNISIA

WESTERN
SAHARA

ALGERIA

LIBYA

EGYPT

MAURITANIA

MALI

SENEGAL
GAMBIA
GUINEA BISSAU

GUINEA

BURKINA

NIGER

CHAD

SUDAN

ERITREA

DJIBOUTI

SIERRA LEONE

IVORY
COAST

NIGERIA

Lake Chad

River Niger

River Nile

ETHIOPIA

LIBERIA

GHANA
TOGO
BENIN

EQUATORIAL
GUINEA

CAMEROON

GABON

CONGO

CENTRAL
AFRICAN REPUBLIC

River Zaire

ZAIRE

UGANDA

RWANDA

BURUNDI

Lake
Turkana

SOMALIA

KENYA

Lake Victoria

Lake Tanganyika

TANZANIA

ANGOLA

ZAMBIA

MALAWI

Lake Nyasa

Indian
Ocean

South Atlantic
Ocean

ZIMBABWE

MADAGASCAR

NAMIBIA

BOTSWANA

MOZAMBIQUE

SWAZILAND

SOUTH
AFRICA

LESOTHO

N

W

S

Range of the chimpanzee

Surrounding land

Sea

Borders

Rivers

A quick look at chimpanzees

What do chimpanzees look like?

Chimpanzees are small apes. Apes do not have tails, but monkeys do. Chimpanzees have short legs and long arms. Their faces are flat and bare. Thick black hair covers most of their bodies.

Where do chimpanzees live?

Chimpanzees live in the forests, rainforests and savannah of western and central Africa.

What do chimpanzees eat?

Chimpanzees eat mostly fruit, nuts and leaves. They sometimes eat other animals, including lizards, birds, monkeys and small pigs.

This chimpanzee is holding its food in its hand.

Chimpanzees in the rainforest

Chimpanzees are mammals. A mammal is a warm-blooded animal with a backbone. Female mammals give birth to live young and feed them with milk from their bodies. Warm-blooded animals have a body temperature that stays the same, no matter what the temperature is outside.

The scientific name for chimpanzees is *Pan troglodytes*. Pan is the name of a Greek god who was part man and part animal. Early travellers to Africa saw wild chimpanzees and thought that this description fitted them well. Troglodyte means 'cave dweller'.

Chimpanzees belong to the **primate** family, along with monkeys and gorillas. All primates are mammals that have large brains and hands that can grasp and hold objects.

 These chimpanzees are knuckle walking.

What do chimpanzees look like?

Chimpanzees are small apes. Male chimpanzees grow up to about 1.2 metres tall. They can weigh up to 60 kilograms. Female chimpanzees are smaller. They are about 0.9 metres tall and usually weigh less than 45 kilograms.

Chimpanzees have flat faces. Their skin colour ranges from pinkish to black. Young chimpanzees have paler skin. It gets darker as they grow older.

A coat of thick, black hair covers most of chimpanzees' bodies. No hair grows on the palms of their hands or the bottom of their feet. Their ears and faces are usually bare too.

The colour of a chimpanzee's hair shows its age. Young chimpanzees have white hair on their buttocks, which disappears when they grow older. Older chimpanzees may have patches of grey hair on their bodies.

A chimpanzee's arms are much longer than its legs. It uses them to climb trees and swing from branch to branch. Long arms are also useful for reaching fruits that grow on high, thin branches.

Chimpanzees have **opposable** thumbs. This means they can place their thumbs against their other fingers. The chimpanzees can hold objects between their thumbs and fingers. Chimpanzees have opposable big toes too.

Chimpanzees usually walk on their knuckles with the back of their hands touching the ground. This is called knuckle walking. They can also walk upright.

Where do chimpanzees live?

Wild chimpanzees live only in Africa. They are found in about 20 different countries from the western coast to as far east as Tanzania.

Most chimpanzees live in forests or rainforests. Rainforests are warm places where many trees and plants grow close together, and rain falls nearly every day.

Although most chimpanzees live in rainforests, they can also live in drier **habitats**. A habitat is a place where an animal or plant usually lives. They may live in drier forests and grassland areas. Because chimpanzees eat many kinds of things, they can live in different habitats. Chimpanzees in dry places eat different kinds of plants to the fruits and plants that grow in the rainforests.

Chimpanzees are social animals, which means they live together in groups. A group of between 15 and 120 chimpanzees is called a community. The community is made up of smaller parties of six or fewer chimpanzees. Parties eat, sleep and travel together. Chimpanzees usually stay with the community in which they were born. But throughout their lives they often change parties.

▲ **Many chimpanzees live in and around rainforest trees.**

A community has its own home range. This is the space where an animal or group of animals lives most of its life. The size of the home range depends on how many chimpanzees live in the community. To protect the home range, male chimpanzees will fight chimpanzees from other communities if they try to enter.

▲ **This chimpanzee is making a face to show his rank.**

Rank

All the chimpanzees in one community know each other. Each chimpanzee has a special rank, or position in the community. All the members of a community know the rank of the other members. Those with higher ranks have more power in the community. They get to mate with the females and eat whatever food they want.

All male chimpanzees are ranked higher than all females. The highest-ranking chimpanzee in the community is called the alpha male. The alpha male often puts on a show to remind everyone that he is the boss. He may break off a tree branch and shake it wildly. Then he may jump around and scream.

Male chimpanzees often fight each other. After a fight, the winner is ranked higher than the loser.

Communication

Chimpanzees can communicate very well with each other. Communicate means to send and receive messages. Chimpanzees communicate with noises and gestures. Gestures are signs made with the hands, face or body.

Chimpanzees make pant-hoots. A pant-hoot starts with a series of short, soft calls that sound like 'ohh' and builds-up to fast, loud sounds. Chimpanzees also make a special screaming sound that warns other chimpanzees of danger.

Chimpanzees use a lot of gestures to communicate with each other. They may hold out their hands, turn around, make faces and even kiss other chimpanzees.

This chimpanzee has used a stick to get honey. It is licking the honey off the stick.

What chimpanzees eat

Chimpanzees are **omnivores**. This means they eat both plants and animals. In the rainforest, chimpanzees eat mostly fruits, nuts, seeds, flowers and leaves. Two of their favourite foods are figs and palm nuts.

Sometimes there is more fruit in the rainforest than usual. This happens because of **mast fruiting**. Mast fruiting is when most of the fruit trees grow fruit at the same time. This happens about every three to seven years. Food is easier for chimpanzees to find at this time.

Chimpanzees also eat other animals. They eat insects, such as ants and termites. Sometimes they eat birds and small mammals they have hunted and killed. They kill animals any way they can. For example, they may squeeze the neck of an animal until it dies.

These chimpanzees are sharing food with each other.

Finding food

Chimpanzees are among the few animals that make and use tools. They may use rocks to crack open nutshells. Then they use their fingers to scoop out the soft insides to eat.

Sometimes chimpanzees use tools to catch insects. To make a tool, a chimpanzee pulls all the leaves off a vine or a twig. Then it places the twig into a termite or ant nest. The insects climb on to it. When the chimpanzee pulls the twig out of the nest, it may have lots of insects to eat. It sucks the insects off the twig. The chimpanzee uses the twig again to catch more insects. It stops eating when it is no longer hungry.

Parties of chimpanzees move around the rainforest to find food. The leader of the party is a male. He pant-hoots so that other members of the group can follow him as he moves through the rainforest. The group looks for ripe fruit or small animals, such as monkeys, lizards and pigs. They chase any small animal they see. If they can catch an animal, they will eat it.

Chimpanzees share food with each other. Some scientists believe chimpanzees grunt and bark to let other chimpanzees know they have found food.

Chimpanzees even share food from their mouths. One chimpanzee may be eating something tasty, such as a bird's egg. Then other chimpanzees signal that they want to share. The first chimpanzee will often open its mouth so that the other chimpanzees can take some food.

This female chimpanzee is standing upright, probably to look at something.

A chimpanzee's life cycle

Chimpanzees can mate at any time of the year. Females mate only once every four to five years. Males can mate every year if they can find females to mate with.

Females begin mating when they are about twelve years old. Some of their skin turns bright pink so males know that they are ready to mate.

Male chimpanzees can mate when they are about thirteen years old. But they usually do not rank high enough to attract females until they are about fifteen. The male puts on a show to attract a female. He may jump around, move his arms, throw sticks and scratch the ground.

Sometimes chimpanzees leave their party to mate. They may go to the edge of their home range for a few days or for several months.

Young

A female gives birth about eight months after mating. She usually gives birth to one baby at a time. Some females have twins, but this is very rare.

Newborn chimpanzees weigh about 1.8 kilograms. They are helpless. Their mothers carry them everywhere they go. The mothers feed their babies with milk from their bodies. This is called **nursing**.

As the chimpanzee grows, it travels with its mother and older brothers and sisters. The father stays in the community, but does not help raise his young. The young chimpanzee begins to eat ripe fruit and leaves. When a chimpanzee is about a year old, it starts to play with other young chimpanzees. They tickle, wrestle and chase each other through the rainforest. By doing this, they learn their rank and how to be members of the community.

Chimpanzees stop nursing when they are about four years old. Then they begin to search for food with other family members.

This young chimpanzee is licking dirt off its thumb.

When young chimpanzees are about eight years old, they enter **adolescence**. They might leave their mothers to travel with other parties. During this period, they must show respect to older male chimpanzees, or they may be attacked.

By the age of fifteen, a chimpanzee is fully grown. It then begins mating and starts a family of its own. Chimpanzees can live to be more than 50 years old.

> **Chimpanzees in this group are grooming each other.**

A day in the life of a chimpanzee

Chimpanzees are part **arboreal** and part **terrestrial**. Arboreal means to live in trees. Terrestrial means to live on the ground. Chimpanzees feed in trees during the day and sleep in trees at night. They travel around and rest on the ground in the daytime.

Chimpanzees are **diurnal**. This means they are active during the day, and they sleep at night. A chimpanzee wakes up early in the morning. Usually, it sets off to look for food straight away. If there is a gathering, it stays in one place. A gathering is when most of the community stays together in one place for a few weeks. Gatherings usually happen when there is a lot of one kind of fruit available to eat in one place.

Throughout the day, chimpanzees communicate with members of their party or community. Touching is very important to them. They hug and kiss each other. They also spend a lot of their time grooming each other. To **groom**, they use their fingers to pick or comb through each other's hair. They remove any dirt, insects and dead skin that they find.

Chimpanzees usually rest in the afternoon. During their rest, older chimpanzees groom each other. Young chimpanzees often play together.

At night, chimpanzees bend branches together to make nests to sleep in. They make new nests every night.

This chimpanzee is using a loud pant-hoot to communicate.

The future of chimpanzees

Scientists think that a chimpanzee's body is more like a human being's than any other animal. Because of this, scientists test medicine on chimpanzees. They are trying to understand diseases and how to cure them in people. Some people think it is good to test medicine on chimpanzees because it might save people's lives. Other people think it is bad because it hurts the chimpanzees or may kill them.

Chimpanzees are also used for entertainment. Entertainment is something enjoyable that people do to amuse themselves. People around the world visit zoos to watch chimpanzees. Chimpanzees even star in films. Some people think this is bad because it is not natural for the chimpanzees.

> Wild chimpanzees may have problems finding food if the rainforest is destroyed.

What will happen to chimpanzees?

Chimpanzees in Africa are **endangered**. Endangered means an animal or plant is in danger of dying out. In 1960, there were 1 million wild chimpanzees. Today, there are fewer than 250,000. Without help, chimpanzees could soon become extinct. Extinct means there are no more of that kind of animal alive in the world.

People have taught some chimpanzees to use sign language. Sign language is a language using hand signals. Chimpanzees can use the sign language to communicate with people and with other chimpanzees.

Chimpanzees are in danger because rainforests are being destroyed. People clear the land for farms and use the wood for buildings. Wildfires also burn large parts of the rainforest. Chimpanzees cannot survive without their habitat.

People also hunt wild chimpanzees in Africa. Some people eat them as food. Others try to catch baby chimpanzees to sell. These hunters often kill the mother chimpanzees. Without adult females to have more babies, there will be fewer baby chimpanzees in the future.

People can help save chimpanzees. Today, many are working to improve the way people in science and entertainment treat chimpanzees. Other people have formed groups that protect wild chimpanzees. In most African countries, it is now against the law to hunt chimpanzees.

flat face
see pages 5, 9

opposable thumbs
see page 9

opposable big toes
see page 9

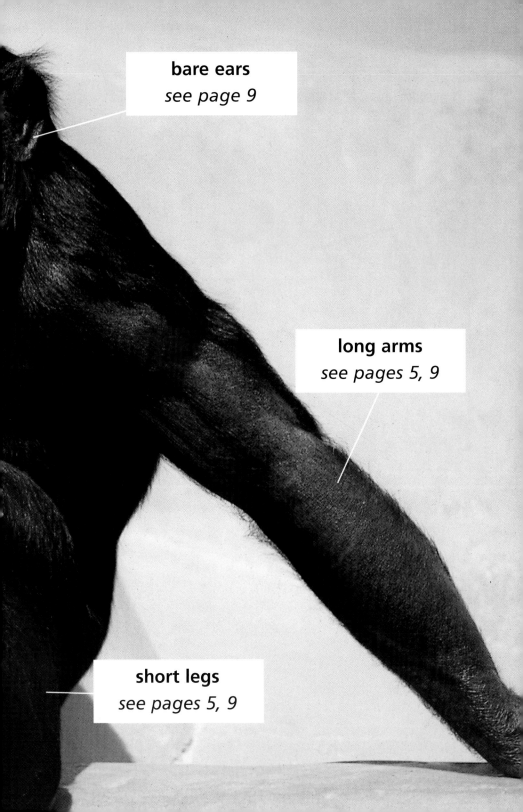

bare ears
see page 9

long arms
see pages 5, 9

short legs
see pages 5, 9

Glossary

adolescence time between childhood and adulthood

arboreal living in trees

diurnal active during the day

endangered animal or plant that is in danger of dying out forever

grooming when an animal cleans its fur or the fur of another animal

habitat place where an animal or plant usually lives

mast fruiting when most of the fruit trees in a large area grow fruit at the same time

nursing when a mother feeds her young milk made inside her body

omnivore animal that eats both plants and animals

opposable ability of thumbs or big toes to be placed against the other fingers or toes

primate mammal that has a large brain and hands that can grasp and hold objects

terrestrial living on the ground

Internet sites

Animals of the Rainforest
www.animalsoftherainforest.org

Jane Goodall Institute
www.janegoodall.org

Useful address

World Wide Fund for Nature – UK
Panda House, Weyside Park
Godalming, Surrey
GU7 1XR

Books to read

Spilsbury, Louise and Richard. *Animal Groups: Life in a troop of Chimpanzees*. Heinemann Library, Oxford, 2003

Robinson, Claire. *Really Wild: Chimpanzees*. Heinemann Library, Oxford, 1997

Index